NEW

CW01663827

Pol and Pax on earth

Hannie Truijens

Illustrated by
John Harrold and Tony Herbert

Nelson

Thomas Nelson and Sons Ltd
Nelson House Mayfield Road
Walton-on-Thames Surrey
KT12 5PL UK

51 York Place
Edinburgh
EH1 3JD UK

Thomas Nelson (Hong Kong) Ltd
Toppan Building 10/F
22A Westlands Road
Quarry Bay Hong Kong

Thomas Nelson Australia
102 Dodds Street
South Melbourne
Victoria 3205 Australia

Nelson Canada
1120 Birchmount Road
Scarborough Ontario
M1K 5G4 Canada

Illustrated by John Harrold and Tony Herbert

First published by Macmillan Education Ltd 1989
ISBN 0-333-48471-1

This edition published by Thomas Nelson and Sons Ltd 1992

ISBN 0-17-400567-9
NPN 9 8 7 6 5 4 3

Printed in Hong Kong

Chapter 1: The space pirate

On a far planet, which turns around a distant sun in another galaxy, live the people of the three moons.

Their planet is not at all like ours. It has three moons and a ring around it. The planet is so cold that the people live underground. They have underground cities, farms, parks and rivers.

The children who live on this planet don't have to go to school. They eat a special brain food every day and this makes them very clever.

Pol and Pax live on the planet of the three moons. They have some very special inventing tools.
They can invent anything they like with these tools. When they get bored they invent something else to do.

"I want to go somewhere else," said Pol. "We've seen all there is to be seen on this planet."

"Let's visit another galaxy," said Pax. "We shall need to make a space craft that can travel faster than time."

Pol and Pax started to invent. They invented for two whole weeks.
Their first space craft was no good and they had to start all over again.
They invented for four whole weeks.

"This space craft will do the trick," said Pax.

They said goodbye to their parents.

"We shall be away for four years," they said, "but when we come back we shall be younger than we are now. This is because we shall be travelling faster than time."

Pol and Pax took off and had soon passed the third moon. "We've left our planet and moons," said Pol. "It's time to go into super-gear."
The space craft went into super-gear and started travelling faster than time.

The first months of the journey went without any trouble. To pass the time they invented a new game every day.
When they were tired of it they threw it out of the space craft.
To this day there are still hundreds of toys and games in space.

At the end of the first year they ran into trouble.

"What's that on your scanner?" asked Pol.

"I'm not sure," said Pax, "but it looks like a space craft to me."
The strange space craft came closer and closer. It didn't look very friendly.

"Let's get out of here," shouted Pol.
He put the space craft into super-super-gear, which was to be used only when they were in trouble.

Their space craft went twice as fast as time but it didn't help them. The strange space craft could travel even faster than that.

A giant claw reached out and captured their craft. Pol and Pax could do nothing about it.

"Let's hope they're friendly," said Pax.

"Not much hope of that," said Pol. "Hide your inventing tools in your space suit. We may need them."

The claw pulled them into the hatch of the pirate craft. "Open your craft or we will blast a hole through it," said a voice.

"We'd better do what they say," said Pax. They opened their craft and were faced with two robots.

"Come with us to our master," they said in tinny voices. Pol and Pax followed the robots to the control room of the pirate craft.

"Well, well, what have we caught here?" said the pirate.

The pirate was the only person in the pirate craft. All his work was done by robots.

"They never give me any trouble," said the pirate, "and that's the way I like it. Where do you come from?"

Pol and Pax told the pirate that they were from the planet of the three moons. "Have you got any gold on your planet?" asked the pirate. Pol and Pax looked at each other. They had never heard of gold.

The pirate showed them a piece of gold. "This is gold," he said, "lovely, hard, cold gold. And I want as much of it as I can get. Now, if you two had some gold," he went on, "I would be happy to take it from you and let you go."

Pol and Pax looked at each other again. "We have lots of gold in our craft," they said, "but you must tell all your robots to help us carry it out."

The pirate ordered all his robots to go with Pol and Pax.

Pol and Pax quickly invented a super-special metal changer. They told the robots to go inside the metal changer to fetch the gold. The metal changer turned the robots into gold pieces and spat out all the wiring. Soon there wasn't a robot left.

They went to call the pirate. "Your gold is here," they said. The pirate couldn't believe his eyes.

"I release you," he said. "Get into your craft and I will push the button to let you out."

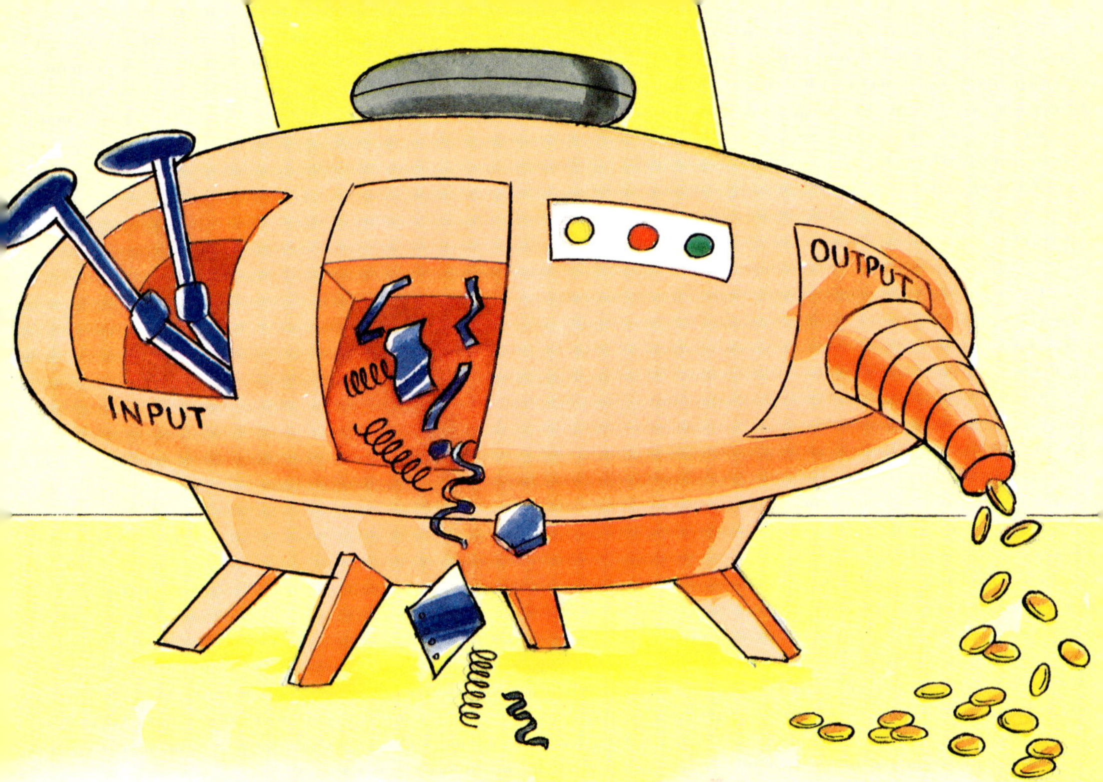

Pol and Pax sped off in their craft.
The pirate kept on counting the gold.
Then he called his robots to help him pack it away.
There wasn't a robot to be found.
The pirate never found out what happened to them. Without his robots he couldn't fly his craft, and he spent the rest of his life drifting in space.

If someone ever finds the pirate craft they will find only a skeleton inside it ... and a pile of gold.

Chapter 2: A strange world

It took Pol and Pax another year to get to the next galaxy. The first sun they came to had many planets around it.
They sent out their heat scanners to find out how hot the planets were.
Some of them were too hot and some of them were too cold, but one of them was just right.

Pol and Pax looked down on a strange world. The skies and the seas were blue.
It had no ring and only one moon.

"It looks all right to me," said Pol.

"I hope the people are friendly," said Pax, "and not like that pirate."

They flew around the earth a few times and then decided where they would land. They chose a small island with no people on it.

"Here we will have time to get used to the air," said Pax.

"And we can also hide our space craft," said Pol.

Pol and Pax spent a week on the island to get used to the air. They tried the food but didn't like it at all.

"You could break your teeth on this stuff," said Pax.

"It's time to meet the people," said Pol. "We shall need a ship to cross this big sea." They invented a super-safe sea boat then loaded up some brain food and their inventing tools. Then they set off across the big blue sea.

They saw the strangest fish they had ever seen in their lives.

"I wonder if there are any sea snakes here," said Pol.

"And if they are as long as our sea snakes," added Pax.

Soon Pol and Pax came to a bigger island. They hid their boat in a cave and climbed up the rocks.

There they saw their first earth people.

"Oh, they look like us," said Pax, "but they are taller and thinner, and rather ugly."

Pol and Pax wanted to get to a big city.
"We shall need something to travel in," said Pol.
"Let's invent something like that," said Pax, pointing to a train. They invented a super-light train for two and drove it along the rails.
They nearly caused an accident.
"Dangerous way of travelling," said Pol.
They came to a city and left their train at the station.

In the city they saw people moving about in cars. "We'll need something like that," said Pax.

"But let's invent one that doesn't smell so," said Pol.

They invented a super-clean car and drove up to a big hotel.

"We want to have a room for two," said Pol to the girl at the desk. She looked at them in surprise but they seemed friendly, so she gave them a room.

Pol and Pax walked or drove around the city, looking at all the things they had never seen before.

"Their way of inventing isn't quite the same as ours," said Pax.

"Yes," said Pol, "they do things the hard way here."

One day Pol and Pax went to see a film about space. They looked at the screen and started laughing.

"It doesn't look like that," said Pol. "Let's show them what it does look like."

Pol and Pax quickly invented a super-clear memory projector and projected their memories onto the screen. They showed the space pirate in his control room.
They showed the robots going into the metal changer. They showed the ring and the moons around their planet.

The people in the hall loved the memory film. "This is the best film on space we have ever seen," they said.
The man in the projecting room couldn't understand it.

Pol and Pax got tired of the city and wanted to leave. They had to pay the hotel, so they quickly invented a super-crisp money printer.
They printed all the money they needed, paid the hotel bill and left with their inventing tools. They got into their car and drove to a smaller town.

"This looks like a nice place," said Pol.

"And it's not as dirty as the big city," said Pax. They looked for a small hotel.

Chapter 3: At school

The next morning Pol and Pax drove around the town. They came to a big building with lots of rooms.
All the rooms were empty.

"That's strange," said Pol, "they have made lots of rooms but nobody lives in them. What a waste of space."

"Let's go out and have a look," said Pax.

They parked their car and walked around the school. Soon lots of children started to pour into the building.

"I wonder what all those children are going to do in there," said Pol.

"Perhaps they are going to get their slice of brain food," said Pax. Pol and Pax looked at each other.

"What are we waiting for?" they said. "Let's go inside and have a look."

Pol and Pax went into one of the rooms. All the children were sitting at little tables. Pol and Pax went to the back of the room and also sat down.

A bell rang and a man walked into the room. “Good morning children,” he said.

“Who’s that?” asked Pol and Pax.

“That’s our teacher,” said a girl sitting next to Pol.

Pol and Pax looked at each other. They had never heard of a teacher before.

“I see we have two new children,” said the teacher. “What are your names?”

Pol and Pax told the teacher their names and the class started. It was the strangest thing that had ever happened to Pol and Pax.

Soon Pol and Pax understood that the teacher was trying to make the children learn. What a strange way to become clever, they thought. It takes a lot more time than eating brain food.

At break Pol and Pax went outside with the children of the class.

"Don't you have any sandwiches?" asked one of the children.

"No, this is our food," said Pax.

"Can I taste some of it?" asked one of the girls. Pol and Pax let all the children taste their brain food.

The children went back into the classroom. The teacher started to teach but all the children already knew the answers. The brain food had started to work, and it works very fast on earth children. The teacher was very surprised.

Pol and Pax laughed. They knew what had happened.

At dinner time the children begged Pol and Pax for some more brain food. They had to go to their car to get some more. All the children got a big slice.

That afternoon there was a terrible accident at the school. A fire broke out in the basement and before anyone knew it the whole building was full of smoke. The caretaker rang the alarm and called the fire brigade.

The children in the top classrooms couldn't get out of the building.

"Don't panic," cried the teachers.

"We must invent something," said Pol.

"And we'd better do it quickly," said Pax.

Pol and Pax took out their inventing tools and started to invent. They invented a super-safe escape chute so that everyone could get out of the building. Then they invented a super-fast fire fighter and put out the fire in the basement in no time at all.

By the time the fire brigade came there was no fire and no smoke.

The firemen had never seen such an escape chute or such a fire fighter before. They asked lots of questions.

"I think it's time to leave," said Pax.

"So do I," said Pol. They waved to the children and drove out of the town.

"I'm homesick," said Pol.

"I'm tired of this strange planet," said Pax.

"Let's go home," they both said. They drove to the station and got into their train for two.

To avoid accidents they invented special propellers for their train. Every time a train came from the other direction they flew over it and landed on the tracks on the other side.

At the coast they got their boat out of the cave. They sailed back to the island and were happy to see that their space craft was still in good order.
They got ready for their long journey.

On the way back to their galaxy Pol and Pax had many adventures, but they are too long to be told here.

They nearly ran out of brain food because they had given too much of it away. They were eating their last slice when they saw their planet.

They passed the three moons and the ring and were very happy to see the green sky of their planet. They made a good landing and their parents came running to meet them.

"Home, sweet home," said Pol and Pax.